The Story of ADAM AND EVE

Fifth Ribb
PUBLISHING

This book is dedicated to Elder Michael Hinds, whose guidance has broadened my perspective on this remarkable story and enabled me to perceive its depth beyond mere words.

Copyright © 2023 by Fifth Ribb Publishing, LLC
All Rights Reserved. Printed in the United States of America
This book or any portion thereof may not be reproduced or used in any manner whatsoever without the express written permission of the publisher except for the use of brief quotations in critical articles and book reviews.
Fifth Ribb Publishing, LLC. 6951 Olive Blvd, University City, MO 63130
www.fifthribbpublishing.com

ISBN: 9781736789865

First Edition

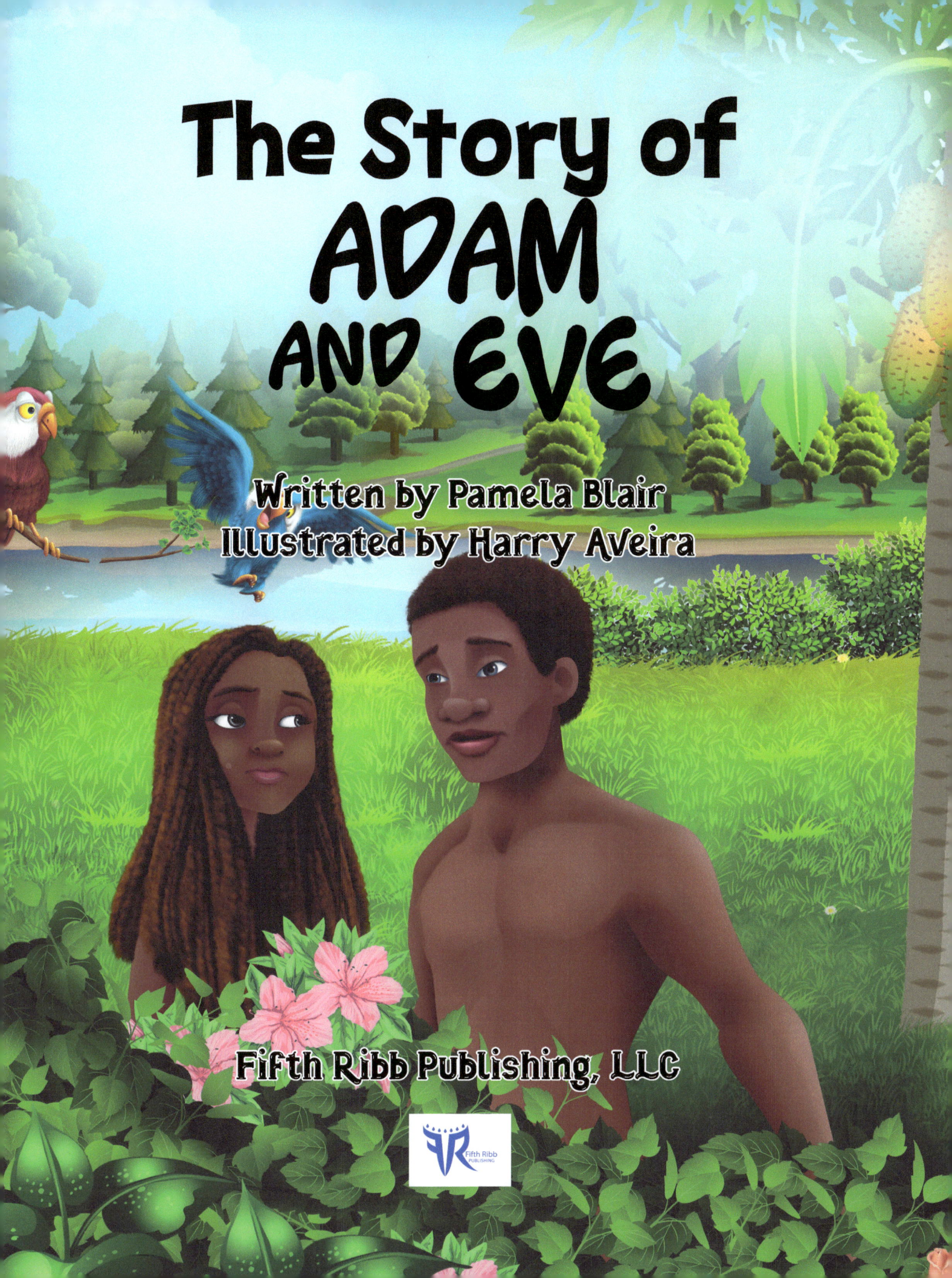

Once upon a time, there were two very special people named Adam and Eve. They were the first man and woman on Earth. Adam and Eve were made by the hands of God. They lived in a beautiful place called the Garden of Eden where they had everything they needed.

The Garden of Eden was filled with colorful flowers that smelled sweet, trees that rustled gently in the breeze, and a soft carpet of grass that tickled their feet.

As the sun shone down, the sound of chirping birds and buzzing insects echoed throughout the Garden. The fruit trees in the Garden were so plentiful that the branches bent low with the weight of the ripe and juicy fruits.

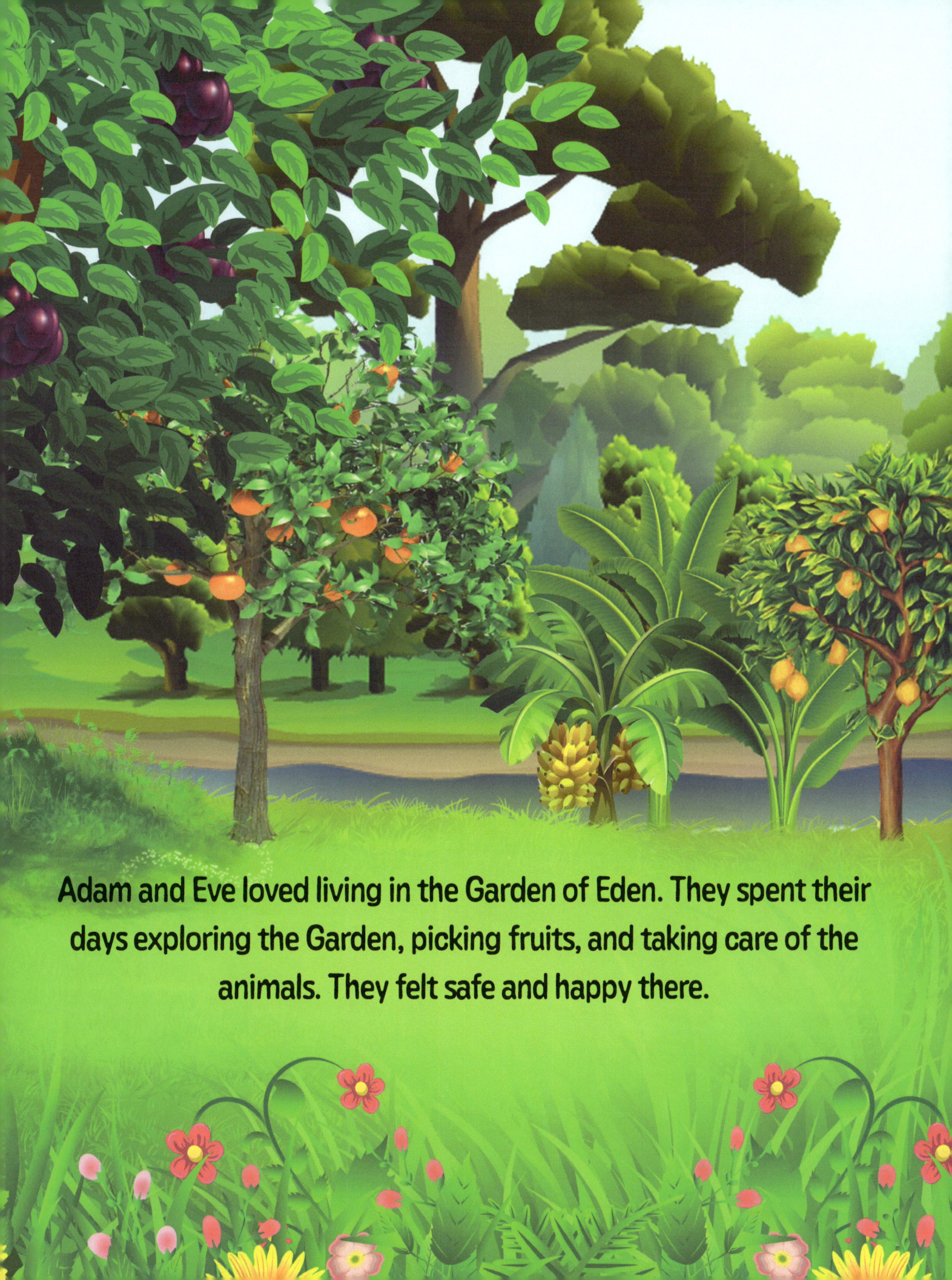

Adam and Eve loved living in the Garden of Eden. They spent their days exploring the Garden, picking fruits, and taking care of the animals. They felt safe and happy there.

One day, a sneaky serpent, adorned with wings, flew into the Garden. His name was Lucifer.

While Adam was playing with the animals, Eve took a walk in the Garden. The serpent talked to her and said, "Hi, Eve! What a pretty garden you have here!"

Eve was enchanted by the serpent. She answered back excitedly, "Thank you! Who are you?"

"I'm a friend," the serpent said. "I have a special fruit from the Tree of Knowledge. If you eat it, you'll become very smart and powerful, like a god."

Eve wasn't sure if she should eat the fruit. God had told them not to eat from the Tree of Knowledge. But the serpent kept telling her it was okay, and Eve really wanted to try it.

So Eve took the fruit and bit into it. Suddenly, she felt very different. Eve now had the understanding of what is good and what is bad.

After they ate the fruit, they started to feel a sense of shame and guilt for disobeying God's command. Adam and Eve knew they had made a mistake, but they couldn't undo what they did. "Adam, I feel terrible," Eve said, tears welling up in her eyes. "We were so foolish to believe the serpent."

Adam put his arm around Eve, trying to comfort her. "I know, Eve. I'm sorry too. We have to face the consequences of our actions. But we can still make things right."

As they heard the sound of God walking in the Garden, they knew they had to face Him. The sound of His footsteps echoed through the trees. Adam and Eve trembled with fear.

God was very upset with them when they told him what happened. He said they had to leave the Garden of Eden forever and go live somewhere else.

Because the serpent tricked Eve, God got angry and took away his wings. Lucifer couldn't fly anymore, and he had to crawl on his belly.

Adam and Eve had to go outside the Garden and find their own food to eat. The Garden of Eden was now guarded by special angels to make sure no one could go back inside.

With a heavy heart, Adam and Eve left the Garden of Eden and had to start a new life.

Despite their regret, Adam and Eve learned from their mistake and tried to make the best of their new life. They always remembered the beauty of the Garden of Eden and hoped to one day find their way back.

Moral

The moral of the story is that sometimes we may be tempted to do things that we know are wrong, but it's important to listen to our inner voice and make the right choices. Even if someone tells us something is okay, we need to think for ourselves and make sure it's the right thing to do. If we make mistakes, we should own up to them and try to make things right again.

Pamela Blair is an acclaimed author renowned for her compelling books inspired by Bible stories. Her writing journey began while homeschooling her children, driven by the desire to impart the knowledge of their biblical heritage. Faced with the absence of illustrated Bible stories featuring children who looked like her own, Pamela took it upon herself to create them.

Prior to delving into the world of Biblical narratives, Pamela earned an undergraduate degree in Business Management from Fairleigh Dickinson University. In addition to her writing endeavors, she is the proud owner of Eyeseeme Bookstore, a distinguished retail establishment that focuses on both fiction and nonfiction narratives celebrating the rich diversity of Black people worldwide.

With a steadfast commitment to family, Pamela has been happily married to Jeffrey Blair for 36 years. Together, they share the joys of parenthood with their four adult children: Jeffrey Jr, Naomi, Sarah, and Ezra. Pamela takes immense pride in her children, attributing their successes to an unwavering faith in God—The God of Abraham, The God of Isaac, and The God of Jacob. This profound spiritual connection has been a guiding light in her family's journey, shaping their lives and achievements.

Through her literary works and her thriving bookstore, Pamela continues to inspire readers and promote inclusivity in storytelling, leaving an indelible mark on the world of literature.

www.ingramcontent.com/pod-product-compliance
Lightning Source LLC
Chambersburg PA
CBHW042147200426
43209CB00065B/1777